Who Is _____?

Your Name Here

The Story of My Life

Who Is _____?

Your Name Here

The Story of My Life

BY PAULA K. MANZANERO

PENGUIN WORKSHOP
AN IMPRINT OF PENGUIN RANDOM HOUSE

FOR IGGY–PM

PENGUIN WORKSHOP
Penguin Young Readers Group
An Imprint of Penguin Random House LLC

Penguin supports copyright. Copyright fuels creativity, encourages diverse voices, promotes free speech, and creates a vibrant culture. Thank you for buying an authorized edition of this book and for complying with copyright laws by not reproducing, scanning, or distributing any part of it in any form without permission. You are supporting writers and allowing Penguin to continue to publish books for every reader.

Photo credits: pages 22–23: © Thinkstock/darksite; page 23: © Thinkstock/tovovan; page 26: © Thinkstock/Inna Afanaseva; page 27: © Thinkstock/StockSolutions; pages 38–39: © Thinkstock/ Andrei Gurov; pages 44–45: © Thinkstock/asmakar; page 53: © Thinkstock/Anna Rassadnikova; page 55: (paper) © Thinkstock/RusN, (rips) © Thinkstock/Mervana; page 57: © Thinkstock/ Giraphics; page 63: © The Museum of Modern Art/Licensed by SCALA/Art Resource, NY; page 66: © Thinkstock/flas100; pages 78–79: © Thinkstock/yukipon.

ISBN 9780448487151   20 19 18 17 16 15

Design Your Cover Art!

Draw a self-portrait in the space below. Cut along the dotted lines. Glue your face onto the cover of this book.

Be creative! Use fabric or yarn to add hair and clothes.

Draw or add details that make this book one of a kind—and all yours!

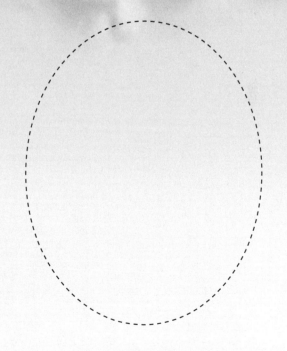

Contents

INTRODUCTION

Let's get started!

A *biography* is the story of a person's life written by another writer. All the books in the Who Was . . . ? series are biographies.

An *autobiography* is the story of a person's life written by that person. In this case: you!

Your personal history belongs to you and only you.

AUTHOR LAURA INGALLS WILDER ONCE SAID . . .

The trouble with organizing a thing is that pretty soon folks get to paying more attention to the organization than to what they're organized for.

The questions in this book will help you tell the unique story of your life. Remember to add as many details as you can. Try not to leave anyone out (BFFs, past friends, teachers, family, or even pets).

If you have trouble starting at the beginning, start in the middle—or even at the end! It's your book, so you can complete it any way you want!

The important thing is simply to get started on the amazing story of you. Get ready to add your name to the list of Who Was . . . ? legends!

THOMAS EDISON MADE OVER ONE THOUSAND UNSUCCESSFUL ATTEMPTS AT INVENTING THE LIGHTBULB BEFORE HE FINALLY GOT IT RIGHT! TALK ABOUT A ROUGH START! WHEN ASKED ABOUT IT, EDISON SAID . . .

I know several thousand things that won't work.

THEN (My Past)

I was born on _____

(date)

in _____ , _____ , _____.

(town/city)   (state)   (country)

I weighed _____ pounds, _____ ounces,

and was _____ inches long.

4

My parents' names are

_____

_____

The people in my family are

_____

_____

_____

_____

ABIGAIL ADAMS WAS NOT ONLY
THE WIFE OF THE SECOND
PRESIDENT OF THE UNITED
STATES, JOHN ADAMS, BUT ALSO
THE MOTHER OF THE SIXTH US
PRESIDENT, JOHN QUINCY ADAMS!

Are you named after anyone? _____

Are you a "Junior," "the Second," or even "the Third"? _____

If you could change your name, what would you change it to? _____

HARRY HOUDINI WAS BORN EHRICH WEISS. PEOPLE CALLED HIM "EHRIE" AND EVENTUALLY "HARRY." HE CHOSE "HOUDINI" TO HONOR THE FRENCH MAGICIAN JEAN-EUGENE ROBERT-HOUDIN.

What is/are/were your nickname(s)?

_____

_____

_____

SIOUX CHIEF SITTING BULL WAS NICKNAMED "SLOW" BECAUSE, EVEN AS A TODDLER, HE NEVER DID ANYTHING QUICKLY.

THEODOR SEUSS GEISEL, ALSO KNOWN AS DR. SEUSS, HAD A SISTER NAMED MARGARETHA. BUT SHE GAVE HERSELF THE NICKNAME "MARNIE MECCA DING DING GUY"!

MARTIAL-ARTS MASTER BRUCE LEE'S NICKNAME WAS "MO SI TING," WHICH MEANT "NEVER SITS STILL"!

Family Tree

GREAT-GRANDMOTHER   GREAT-GRANDFATHER   GREAT-GRANDMOTHER   GREAT-GRANDFATHER

GRANDMOTHER   GRANDFATHER

MOM

ME

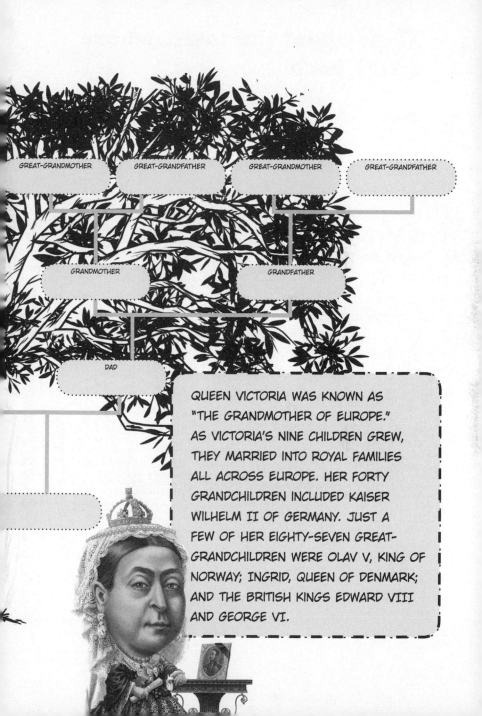

GREAT-GRANDMOTHER

GREAT-GRANDFATHER

GREAT-GRANDMOTHER

GREAT-GRANDFATHER

GRANDMOTHER

GRANDFATHER

DAD

QUEEN VICTORIA WAS KNOWN AS "THE GRANDMOTHER OF EUROPE." AS VICTORIA'S NINE CHILDREN GREW, THEY MARRIED INTO ROYAL FAMILIES ALL ACROSS EUROPE. HER FORTY GRANDCHILDREN INCLUDED KAISER WILHELM II OF GERMANY. JUST A FEW OF HER EIGHTY-SEVEN GREAT-GRANDCHILDREN WERE OLAV V, KING OF NORWAY; INGRID, QUEEN OF DENMARK; AND THE BRITISH KINGS EDWARD VIII AND GEORGE VI.

Facts about the town where I was born

_____

_____

Best park to play in _____

Streets named after

Trees _____

Presidents _____

Flowers _____

Directions (North, South, East, West)

_____

Something else _____

Facts about the state where I was born

State capital _____

State bird _____

State flower _____

State tree _____

State song _____

A famous person from my state is

_____

Favorite things when I was little (the baby years)

Favorite stuffed animal(s)

_____

_____

_____

Favorite board book(s)

_____

_____

_____

Favorite toy(s)

_____

_____

_____

_____

Favorite things when I was a little bigger (the toddler years)

I always slept with

_____

_____

Favorite picture book(s)

_____

_____

Favorite toy(s)

_____

_____

Do you still have your favorites?

AS A YOUNG GIRL, SCIENTIST JANE GOODALL DUG UP SOME EARTHWORMS FROM HER YARD AND PUT THEM UNDER HER PILLOW! HER MOTHER EXPLAINED THAT EARTHWORMS NEED TO STAY IN THEIR OWN HOMES IN THE GROUND—OUTSIDE THE HOUSE!

First school _____

First teacher _____

The friends I met the very first day of school

_____

_____

_____

_____

_____

_____

_____

_____

Best kindergarten friends

_____

_____

_____

_____

_____

My BFFs from first grade

_____

_____

_____

_____

_____

What is the biggest challenge you had to overcome when you were younger?

☐ Learning to read?

☐ Learning to ride a bike?

☐ Learning to swim?

☐ _____

☐ _____

☐ _____

SOME PEOPLE BELIEVE THAT FAMOUS PHYSICIST ALBERT EINSTEIN DIDN'T SPEAK A WORD UNTIL HE WAS FOUR YEARS OLD. MANY OF HIS TEACHERS THOUGHT HE WAS LAZY AND WOULDN'T AMOUNT TO MUCH. HE EVEN FAILED TO GET INTO COLLEGE ON HIS FIRST TRY. EINSTEIN WENT ON TO DEVELOP THE THEORY OF RELATIVITY AND TO BECOME ONE OF THE GREATEST MINDS OF THE TWENTIETH CENTURY.

How did you overcome your biggest challenge?

_____

_____

_____

Do you have a secret strategy or advice for others?

_____

_____

_____

FOR DECADES, NEW YORK YANKEE BABE RUTH HELD THE RECORD FOR MOST STRIKEOUTS—1,330 IN ALL! HE WAS NEVER DISCOURAGED, THOUGH. HE SAID THAT "EVERY STRIKE BRINGS ME CLOSER TO THE NEXT HOME RUN." RUTH BECAME KNOWN AS THE HOME RUN KING, AND HIS CAREER TOTAL OF HOME RUNS, 714, WAS A RECORD THAT LASTED UNTIL 1974.

NOW (My Present)

I used to be totally into _____,

(monster trucks and unicorns?)

but I'm over it:

_____

_____

_____

_____

_____

_____

_____

_____

18

Now I'm totally into _____:

(monster trucks and unicorns?)

_____

_____

_____

_____

_____

_____

_____

ORVILLE AND WILBUR WRIGHT WERE
TOTALLY INTO BUILDING AND SELLING
BICYCLES BEFORE THEY BEGAN THEIR
EXPERIMENTS WITH FLYING MACHINES.

Status Update!

Where do you live now?

_____

Where do you go to school?

_____

PIONEER LEADER DANIEL BOONE'S MOST IMPORTANT TEACHERS WERE THE DELAWARE INDIANS. THEY TAUGHT HIM HUNTING AND TRACKING SKILLS AND HOW TO SURVIVE IN THE FOREST.

My teacher

_____

My current grade

_____

My classroom number

_____

ABRAHAM LINCOLN ONLY
COMPLETED A TOTAL OF ABOUT
ONE YEAR OF FORMAL SCHOOLING
IN HIS LIFETIME. HE WAS MOSTLY
SELF-TAUGHT. WHEN HE WAS
YOUNG, HE WOULD PRACTICE
WRITING WITH A PIECE OF
CHARCOAL OR INK MADE FROM
BLACKBERRY JUICE!

21

Map your neighborhood! (Your house, your block, your secret spaces . . .)

My Pets

_____

_____

_____

THESE ARE ONLY *SOME* OF THE PETS THAT PRESIDENT THEODORE ROOSEVELT'S CHILDREN KEPT WHILE LIVING IN THE WHITE HOUSE:

DOGS:	JACK, SAILOR BOY, GEM, SUSAN, RONALD, ALLAN, MANCHU, PETE, ROLLO, AND SKIP
CATS:	TOM QUARTZ AND SLIPPERS
HORSES:	YAGENKA, JOCKO ROOT, RENOWN, ALGONQUIN, BLEISTEIN, AND WYOMING
HENS:	BARON SPECKLE AND FIERCE
RABBIT:	PETER
MACAW:	ELI YALE
PIG:	MAUDE
BEAR:	JONATHAN EDWARDS
GUINEA PIGS:	ADMIRAL DEWEY, BISHOP DOANE, DR. JOHNSON, FATHER O'GRADY, AND FIGHTING BOB EVANS
BADGER:	JOSIAH

Pet Cemetery

Pets I've lost

_____

_____

_____

_____

_____

Pets I wish I had

_____

_____

_____

Take a break! Doodle!

BFs

_____

_____

_____

DIRECTORS GEORGE LUCAS AND
STEVEN SPIELBERG, FRIENDS
SINCE THE 1960S, DREAMED
UP THE IDEA FOR THE INDIANA
JONES MOVIES WHILE ON
VACATION TOGETHER IN HAWAII.

DIRECTOR

BFFs

_____

_____

_____

_____

28

Friends' nicknames

_____

_____

_____

Do you know how they got those nicknames?

_____

_____

_____

ARTIST FRIDA KAHLO'S PARENTS CALLED HER AND HER HUSBAND, DIEGO RIVERA, "THE DOVE AND THE ELEPHANT" BECAUSE SHE WAS SO TINY AND HE WAS SO LARGE!

My favorite home-cooked meal

_____

_____

_____

_____

_____

_____

_____

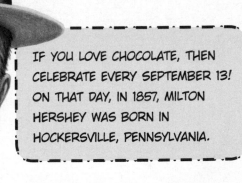

IF YOU LOVE CHOCOLATE, THEN CELEBRATE EVERY SEPTEMBER 13! ON THAT DAY, IN 1857, MILTON HERSHEY WAS BORN IN HOCKERSVILLE, PENNSYLVANIA.

Recipe for my favorite meal

FRENCH IMPRESSIONIST ARTIST CLAUDE MONET'S FAVORITE DISH WAS RED BEANS COOKED IN WINE. HE ALSO LIKED GOOSE LIVER!

Favorite snacks

_____

_____

_____

_____

_____

_____

_____

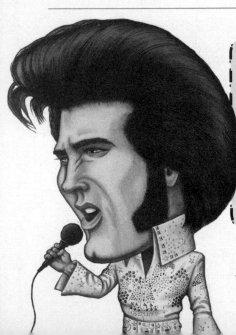

"THE ELVIS" IS ONE OF THE MOST WELL-KNOWN CELEBRITY SANDWICHES IN THE UNITED STATES. THE KING OF ROCK 'N' ROLL'S FAVORITE SNACK WAS A FRIED PEANUT-BUTTER-AND-BANANA SANDWICH, SOMETIMES WITH BACON!

Best school-lunch food ever

Worst school-lunch food disaster you wouldn't even serve to a dog

---

MOHANDAS GANDHI, LEADER OF THE INDIAN INDEPENDENCE MOVEMENT AND LIFELONG VEGETARIAN, HAD A CHILDHOOD FRIEND WHO TOLD HIM THAT EATING MEAT WOULD MAKE HIM BRAVE! BUT IT ONLY MADE HIM SICK; HE WAS BRAVE ENOUGH WITHOUT IT!

Go Team!

My favorite teams

_____

_____

_____

_____

_____

My favorite players

_____

_____

_____

_____

Sports I play

_____

_____

_____

Teams I've played on

_____

_____

_____

Sports I like to watch

_____

_____

BY AGE TEN, ICE-HOCKEY LEGEND WAYNE
GRETZKY HAD SCORED AN ASTONISHING
378 GOALS IN JUST *ONE SEASON* WITH
HIS ONTARIO TEAM, THE BRANTFORD
NADROFSKY STEELERS!

What's in your junk drawer?

What do you collect?

_____

_____

_____

_____

_____

_____

_____

_____

WORLD TRAVELER ROBERT RIPLEY
COLLECTED TORTURE DEVICES,
SHRUNKEN HEADS, WACKY ART, TRIBAL
WEAPONS, ANCIENT MASKS, AND
AMAZING HUMAN TALENTS, RECORDS,
AND STUNTS! *BELIEVE IT OR NOT!*

Map your room

EVEN THOUGH EXPLORER FERDINAND MAGELLAN USED A LEATHER GLOBE IN 1518 TO CONVINCE THE KING OF SPAIN TO FINANCE HIS AROUND-THE-WORLD VOYAGE, MANY OF HIS OWN CREWMEN STILL BELIEVED THAT THE WORLD WAS FLAT. THEY FEARED THEY WERE DOOMED TO SAIL OVER THE EARTH'S EDGE!

Favorite singer

_____

Favorite group

_____

Favorite lyrics

_____

_____

_____

_____

_____

_____

40

My band would be

- [ ] Rock
- [ ] Country
- [ ] Rap
- [ ] Pop
- [ ] Hip-hop
- [ ] Orchestra

- [ ] Marching band
- [ ] School band
- [ ] Punk
- [ ] Metal
- [ ] Funk

Instrument I play _____

Instrument I *wish* I played

_____

BOB DYLAN TAUGHT HIMSELF
TO PLAY THE PIANO WHEN HE
WAS ONLY TEN!

Write a poem!

A haiku is a poem written in a Japanese style that does not rhyme.

It has three lines; the first has five syllables, the second has seven syllables, and the third has five syllables.

Here is a sample haiku:

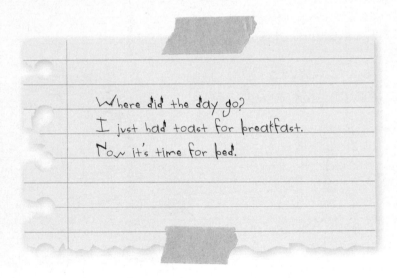

Where did the day go?
I just had toast for breakfast.
Now it's time for bed.

Now write your own haiku!

Haiku of My Life

_____

_____

_____

_____

_____

_____

_____

_____

_____

_____

_____

My Artistic Side

WHEN ARTIST PABLO PICASSO WAS A YOUNG MAN, HE MOVED TO PARIS. HE HAD NO MONEY TO BUY FURNITURE, SO HE PAINTED FURNITURE AND BOOKCASES ON THE WALLS OF HIS APARTMENT! HE EVEN PAINTED A SAFE ON THE WALL, AS THOUGH HE HAD VALUABLE THINGS TO PUT IN IT!

Favorite superhero(es)

_____

_____

_____

_____

What would your superhero powers be?

_____

_____

_____

THE MAN BEHIND MARVEL COMICS, STAN LEE, SAID THAT HE CAME UP WITH THE IDEA FOR SPIDER-MAN AFTER WATCHING A FLY CLIMB UP A WALL. HE LIKED THE IDEA OF A SUPERHERO WHO COULD STICK TO THINGS, BUT FLY-MAN AND INSECT-MAN JUST DIDN'T SOUND RIGHT!

List all your minions, henchmen, sidekicks, and assistants here

_____

_____

_____

List all your vehicles, gadgets, and weapons here

_____

_____

_____

THE BOY PHARAOH, KING TUT,
HAD GUARDS WHO KEPT WATCH
FOR CROCODILES EVERY TIME
HE SWAM IN THE NILE RIVER.
HE ALSO HAD A SCRIBE TO WRITE
ALL HIS LETTERS FOR HIM!

Favorite games to play outside (capture the flag, anyone?)

_____

_____

_____

_____

_____

_____

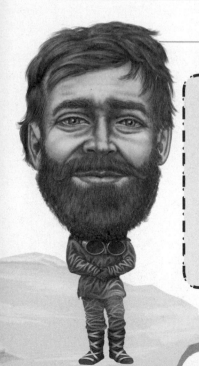

WHEN ANTARCTIC EXPLORER ERNEST SHACKLETON WAS FIVE YEARS OLD, HE LOVED TO STAND ON THE GIANT TRUNK OF A FALLEN TREE IN HIS YARD AND PRETEND HE WAS CAPTAIN OF A GREAT SHIP! YEARS LATER, HE CAPTAINED NOT ONE BUT TWO SHIPS ON FAMOUS VOYAGES TO THE SOUTH POLE: THE *NIMROD* AND THE *ENDURANCE*.

Favorite games to play inside (video games, board games, card games . . .)

_____

_____

_____

_____

_____

_____

_____

_____

_____

The perfect sleepover

Food _____

Game _____

Theme _____

Things to do _____

_____

_____

Rules
(There are no rules!)

_____

_____

_____

_____

The best night of my life

_____

_____

_____

_____

_____

_____

SCIENTIST CHARLES DARWIN'S
TRIP AROUND THE WORLD ON
THE *BEAGLE* TOOK FIVE LONG
YEARS! ABOARD THE SHIP, HE
SHARED A SMALL ROOM, CALLED
A "POOP CABIN," WITH TWO
OFFICERS. THE ROOM WAS SO
CRAMPED, HE HAD TO REMOVE A
DRAWER IN THE WALL SO THAT
HIS FEET COULD HANG OVER THE
END OF HIS SLEEP HAMMOCK!
TALK ABOUT CLOSE QUARTERS!

What is the grossest thing you've ever done? _____

_____

_____

_____

The grossest thing you've ever eaten? _____

_____

_____

The grossest thing you've ever smelled? _____

_____

_____

What is the grossest thing you've ever seen someone else do?

_____

_____

_____

_____

_____

_____

_____

EMPEROR GENGHIS KHAN'S SWIFT-
MOVING MONGOL ARMY NEVER
STOPPED TO REFUEL. EACH MAN
CARRIED ONLY WHAT HE NEEDED.
IF THE MEN RAN OUT OF WATER,
THEY DRANK HORSES' BLOOD
INSTEAD! (GROSS!)

TV Time!

Favorite TV shows

Now

_____

_____

_____

_____

_____

Of all time

_____

_____

_____

_____

_____

Favorite actors and actresses

_____

_____

_____

_____

_____

_____

_____

WHEN MARTIAL-ARTS LEGEND BRUCE LEE BEGAN TAPING HIS TV SHOW, *THE GREEN HORNET,* HE WAS TOO FAST FOR THE CAMERAS TO CATCH ALL HIS INCREDIBLE MOVES! THE PRODUCERS ASKED HIM TO SLOW DOWN HIS CHARACTER KATO'S MARTIAL-ARTS SCENES BECAUSE THEY DIDN'T THINK VIEWERS WOULD BELIEVE ANYONE COULD MOVE THAT FAST!

If Only . . . !
I wish I had

- [ ] A tail
- [ ] A beak
- [ ] Horns
- [ ] Hooves
- [ ] Whiskers
- [ ] _____

- [ ] Fur
- [ ] Fins
- [ ] Gills
- [ ] Scales
- [ ] A unicorn horn
- [ ] _____

ONE OF THE FIRST EUROPEANS TO GLIMPSE A RHINOCEROS, EXPLORER MARCO POLO, THOUGHT THE HORNED ANIMAL WAS A UNICORN! HE ALSO DESCRIBED CROCODILES AS GIANT, SHARP-CLAWED "SERPENTS."

If you could be any animal,
what would it be?_____

Why?_____

_____

Draw yourself as that animal.

Bookshelf
Favorite books

_____

_____

_____

_____

_____

_____

_____

AUTHOR ROALD DAHL WROTE
NEARLY FIFTY BOOKS FOR
BOTH CHILDREN AND ADULTS,
INCLUDING *JAMES AND THE
GIANT PEACH, CHARLIE AND
THE CHOCOLATE FACTORY,
FANTASTIC MR. FOX,* AND
MATILDA.

Favorite book series

_____

_____

_____

_____

_____

_____

_____

J. K. ROWLING WROTE
THE HARRY POTTER
BOOKS. WHEN SHE WAS
GROWING UP, SOME OF
HER FAVORITE BOOKS
WERE *THE CHRONICLES
OF NARNIA* BY C. S.
LEWIS.

Bookshelf Part II!

My own book would be

- ☐ Comic book
- ☐ Chapter book
- ☐ Graphic novel
- ☐ Doodle book
- ☐ Picture book
- ☐ Scrapbook
- ☐ Other_____

JUST A FEW OF PRESIDENT JOHN F. KENNEDY'S FAVORITE BOYHOOD BOOKS WERE *THE ARABIAN NIGHTS, TREASURE ISLAND, THE JUNGLE BOOK, UNCLE TOM'S CABIN,* AND *PETER PAN.*

The title of my book would be _____

_____

It would take place _____

_____

The main characters would be

_____

The plot of my story _____

_____

_____

_____

_____

Things That Creep Me Out

☐ Zombies
☐ Haunted houses
☐ Math tests
☐ Spiders
☐ Snakes
☐ My little brother (or sister or cousin)

_____

_____

_____

_____

_____

_____

_____

DID YOU KNOW THAT THE HOUSE IN THE MOVIE *PSYCHO*, DIRECTED BY HOLLYWOOD LEGEND ALFRED HITCHCOCK, WAS BASED ON A FAMOUS PAINTING? EDWARD HOPPER'S *HOUSE BY THE RAILROAD* (1925) WAS THE INSPIRATION FOR THE HOUSE WHERE NORMAN BATES LIVED BEHIND HIS FAMILY'S ROADSIDE MOTEL. THE *PSYCHO* HOUSE IS STILL A FAVORITE ATTRACTION ON THE UNIVERSAL STUDIOS TOUR.

Save the Planet!

I recycle

- ☐ Paper
- ☐ Glass
- ☐ Plastic
- ☐ Aluminum cans
- ☐ Clothes
- ☐ Books

I . . .

- ☐ Limit water use
- ☐ Ride my bike
- ☐ Take quick showers
- ☐ Drink from a reusable water bottle
- ☐ Don't let the water run when I brush my teeth
- ☐ Carry a reusable shopping bag
- ☐ Eat vegetarian at least once a week

Know Your Environment!

List the trees, plants, flowers, waterways, insects, birds, and animals you can find closest to your home

_____

_____

_____

_____

_____

ENVIRONMENTALIST RACHEL CARSON WAS JUST ONE PERSON, BUT SHE WORKED HARD TO MAKE THE WORLD A CLEANER, BETTER, AND SAFER PLACE. IN 1962, HER BOOK *SILENT SPRING* OPENED THE WORLD'S EYES TO MANY ENVIRONMENTAL ISSUES THAT WERE JUST TOO IMPORTANT TO IGNORE.

Best birthday party you've ever had

_____

_____

_____

_____

_____

_____

_____

_____

ALTHOUGH THE EXACT DATE OF HIS BIRTH IS UNKNOWN, PLAYWRIGHT WILLIAM SHAKESPEARE'S BIRTHDAY IS CELEBRATED ON APRIL 23— ALSO KNOWN AS NATIONAL SHAKESPEARE DAY!

Best birthday party you've ever been to

_____

_____

_____

_____

_____

_____

_____

WOMEN'S RIGHTS ADVOCATE
GLORIA STEINEM CELEBRATED
HER FIFTIETH BIRTHDAY WITH
750 FRIENDS AND GUESTS! THEY
INCLUDED CIVIL RIGHTS PIONEER
ROSA PARKS AND ASTRONAUT
SALLY RIDE.

67

What person in the world would you most like to meet?

Why?

_____

_____

_____

_____

_____

_____

_____

_____

_____

_____

Whose mind do you wish you could read? _____
Why?

_____

_____

What do you wish you could make disappear? _____
Why?

_____

PLENTY OF MAGICIANS MAKE THINGS "DISAPPEAR"—A RABBIT, A COIN, OR EVEN A PERSON. BUT ESCAPE ARTIST HARRY HOUDINI MADE JENNY, A TEN-THOUSAND-POUND ELEPHANT, DISAPPEAR IN HIS ACT "THE VANISHING ELEPHANT." AUDIENCES WERE AMAZED!

69

Do you wear glasses?
If not, draw yourself a pair or two!

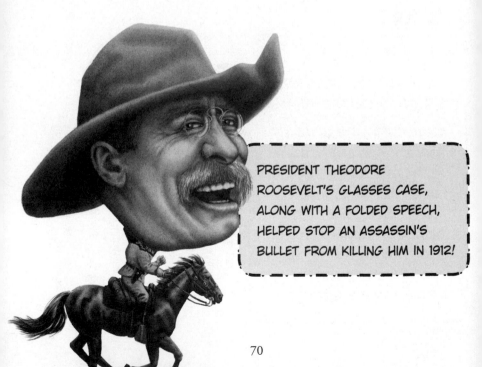

PRESIDENT THEODORE ROOSEVELT'S GLASSES CASE, ALONG WITH A FOLDED SPEECH, HELPED STOP AN ASSASSIN'S BULLET FROM KILLING HIM IN 1912!

Have you ever . . .

☐ Had a broken bone?
☐ Had a cast?
☐ Had to go to the emergency room?
☐ Spent time in the hospital?
☐ Had a sports injury?

Add all the gory details

_____

_____

_____

_____

_____

_____

My favorite jokes

_____

_____

_____

_____

_____

_____

_____

PRESIDENT ABRAHAM LINCOLN WAS KNOWN FOR HIS SENSE OF HUMOR. HERE ARE A FEW OF LINCOLN'S MOST FAMOUS JOKES:

If this is coffee, please bring me some tea; if this is tea, please bring me some coffee.

If I were two-faced, would I be wearing this one?

What are your favorite pranks?

_____

_____

_____

Who do you play pranks on?

_____

_____

_____

WHEN APPLE FOUNDER STEVE JOBS WAS A BOY, HE PASSED OUT FLYERS IN SCHOOL ANNOUNCING "BRING YOUR PET TO SCHOOL DAY"—AN UNOFFICIAL SCHOOL EVENT STEVE INVENTED AS A MAJOR PRANK!

Favorite movie this year

WALT DISNEY'S MOVIE *SNOW WHITE AND THE SEVEN DWARFS* PREMIERED IN DECEMBER 1937. IT WAS THE FIRST FEATURE-LENGTH ANIMATED MOVIE, MADE UP OF OVER 250,000 DRAWINGS! *SNOW WHITE AND THE SEVEN DWARFS* WENT ON TO EARN OVER $400 MILLION AND WIN A SPECIAL ACADEMY AWARD. SINCE THEN, DISNEY STUDIOS HAS MADE OVER FIFTY ANIMATED MOVIES.

Top ten favorite movies of all time

1. _____

2. _____

3. _____

4. _____

5. _____

6. _____

7. _____

8. _____

9. _____

10. _____

Words to Live By!

My motto is _____

_____

_____

STAN LEE'S MOTTO IS
"EXCELSIOR!", WHICH IS ALSO
THE MOTTO OF NEW YORK STATE.
IT MEANS "STILL HIGHER"!

My favorite song to

Sing in the shower _____

Sing with friends _____

Sing in the car _____

My theme song _____

SHARPSHOOTER ANNIE OAKLEY'S MOTTO WAS "AIM AT A HIGH MARK AND YOU WILL HIT IT. NO, NOT THE FIRST TIME, NOR THE SECOND AND MAYBE NOT THE THIRD. BUT KEEP ON AIMING AND KEEP ON SHOOTING FOR ONLY PRACTICE WILL MAKE YOU PERFECT. FINALLY, YOU'LL HIT THE BULL'S-EYE OF SUCCESS."

My Greatest Achievement in Life

_____

_____

_____

_____

_____

_____

_____

_____

_____

_____

_____

BE YOURSELF! DOLLY PARTON LIKES HOW SHE LOOKS: ALTHOUGH SHE IS KNOWN FOR HER CURVY FIGURE, GLITTERY CLOTHES, AND BIG BLOND WIGS, SHE HAS ALWAYS BEEN TRUE TO HERSELF. HER UPBEAT PERSONALITY CHARMS EVERYONE SHE MEETS. THERE IS NO ONE ELSE LIKE HER!

Top five things that make me smile

1. _____

2. _____

3. _____

4. _____

5. _____

What or who inspires you?

_____

_____

_____

_____

_____

_____

WHEN MARTIN LUTHER KING JR. WAS FIFTEEN
YEARS OLD, HE MET DR. BENJAMIN MAYS, A
DISTINGUISHED AFRICAN AMERICAN MINISTER
AND SCHOLAR. DR. MAYS TAUGHT KING ABOUT
GANDHI'S PRINCIPLES OF NONVIOLENT PROTEST
AND THE IMPORTANCE OF UPHOLDING THE
DIGNITY OF ALL HUMAN BEINGS. MAYS WAS AN
INSPIRATION TO KING, AND THE TWO REMAINED
LIFELONG FRIENDS.

My favorite outfit

_____

_____

_____

What did you wear on the first day of school this year?

_____

_____

_____

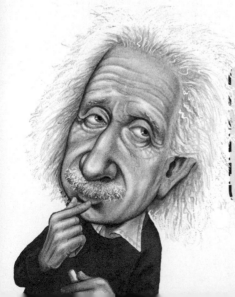

ALBERT EINSTEIN DIDN'T LIKE
TO WEAR SOCKS. HE WAS ALSO
KNOWN TO GO WITHOUT A BELT
OR SUSPENDERS. (HOW DID HE
KEEP HIS PANTS UP?)

82

Draw your favorite T-shirt here!

SOMEDAY
(My Future)

I want to be a/an _____ when I
grow up.

List your top five job choices

1. _____

2. _____

3. _____

4. _____

5. _____

OCEAN EXPLORER JACQUES COUSTEAU ORIGINALLY WANTED TO BE AN AIRPLANE PILOT. AFTER A SERIOUS CAR ACCIDENT, COUSTEAU BEGAN SWIMMING AS THERAPY TO STRENGTHEN HIS ARMS. UNDER THE SEA OFF THE COAST OF FRANCE, HE REALIZED HE HAD FOUND HIS TRUE CALLING.

Draw what you think you will look like when you are thirty!

What will you be doing and where will you be living in twenty years?

IN 1962, WHEN THE BEATLES WERE JUST STARTING OUT, A RECORD-COMPANY EXECUTIVE TOLD THEM GUITAR MUSIC WAS "ON THE WAY OUT." BOY, WAS HE WRONG! ALTHOUGH THE BAND BROKE UP IN 1970, THEY'VE GONE ON TO SELL A WHOPPING SIX HUNDRED MILLION ALBUMS WORLDWIDE!

My dream house

- ☐ Tree house
- ☐ RV
- ☐ Cave
- ☐ Cottage
- ☐ House
- ☐ Penthouse apartment
- ☐ Tent
- ☐ Apartment
- ☐ Barn
- ☐ Lighthouse
- ☐ Shack

_____

_____

_____

_____

Draw your dream house!

My dream vacation

_____

_____

Dream vacation

☐ Sleep until noon every day
☐ Wear pj's for a week
☐ Bike
☐ Hike
☐ Read
☐ Paddle in a pool
☐ Swim in the ocean
☐ Apartment
☐ _____

Camp

☐ Yes!
☐ Never!

Bucket List!

The things I'd like to see and do in my lifetime

_____

_____

_____

_____

_____

_____

WHEN ASTRONAUT SALLY RIDE WAS NINE YEARS OLD, HER PARENTS DECIDED TO TAKE A YEAR OFF AND GO ON A FAMILY ADVENTURE TO EUROPE! THEY BELIEVED THAT TRAVELING AND SEEING THE WORLD WAS JUST AS IMPORTANT AS SCHOOL.

Been There, Done That!

List all the places you've been to.

_____

_____

_____

_____

_____

_____

_____

_____

_____

_____

_____

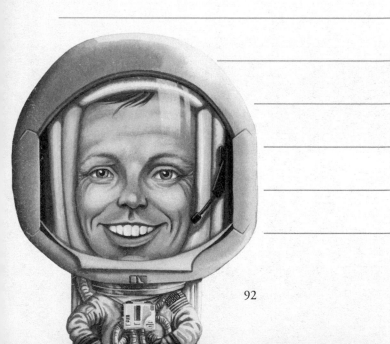

Unexplored Territory!

List all the places you'd like to travel to.

_____

_____

_____

_____

_____

_____

_____

_____

I am brave enough to _____,

_____

_____

_____

_____

_____

_____

but too scared to _____

_____

_____

_____

_____

_____

_____ .

Someday I'll be brave enough to

_____

_____

_____

_____

_____

_____.

WHEN ELEANOR ROOSEVELT WAS A YOUNG WOMAN, SHE WAS TERRIFIED OF DANCES, PARTIES, AND BALLS. SHE FELT LIKE AN UGLY DUCKLING. SHE WAS AFRAID THAT NO ONE WOULD ASK HER TO DANCE! ELEANOR WENT ON TO BECOME A TEACHER, A NEWSPAPER COLUMNIST, AND A BEST-SELLING AUTHOR. SHE WAS ALSO FIRST LADY LONGER THAN ANY OTHER WOMAN IN US HISTORY!

Planning for the Future!

Husband?

☐ Yes
☐ No
☐ Maybe

Wife

☐ Yes
☐ No
☐ Maybe

QUEEN ELIZABETH I WAS THE DAUGHTER OF HENRY VIII. SHE RULED ENGLAND FOR FORTY-FIVE YEARS AND WAS NEVER MARRIED. SHE ONCE DECLARED, "I WOULD RATHER BE A BEGGAR AND SINGLE THAN A QUEEN AND MARRIED!"

How many?

_____ Kids

_____ Dogs

_____ Cats

_____ Cars

_____ Hamsters

_____ Go-carts

_____ Ferris wheels

_____ Boats

_____ Friends

_____ Trampolines

_____ Ferrets

What else?

_____

_____

_____

Message to my future self

Time Capsule!

Today's date _____

At this very moment, my favorites are

Colors _____

Numbers _____

Animals _____

Subjects _____

Places _____

People _____

Sports _____

Games _____

PATRIOT, INVENTOR, AND SCIENTIST BEN FRANKLIN'S FAVORITE SPORTS AS A YOUNG BOY WERE KITE-FLYING AND SWIMMING. HE USED WOODEN PADDLES AS EARLY SWIM FINS TO HELP HIM SWIM FASTER!

The most important thing you should know about me

_____

_____

_____

_____

_____

_____

_____

_____

_____

_____

TIMELINE OF MY LIFE

Begin with the year you were born, and add dates for important events in your life, up to and including the present year.

(20) _____

(20) _____

(20) _____

(20) _____

(20) _____

(20) _____

(20) _____

(20) _____

(20) _____

20 _____

20 _____

20 _____

20 _____

20 _____

20 _____

20 _____

20 _____

20 _____

20 _____

20 _____

20 _____

20 _____

20 _____

TIMELINE OF
THE WORLD

Begin with the year you were born, and add dates for important world events that have happened during your lifetime, up to and including the present year.

(20   ) _____

(20   ) _____

(20   ) _____

(20   ) _____

(20   ) _____

(20   ) _____

(20   ) _____

(20   ) _____

(20   ) _____

(20) _____

(20) _____

(20) _____

(20) _____

(20) _____

(20) _____

(20) _____

(20) _____

(20) _____

(20) _____

(20) _____

(20) _____

(20) _____

(20) _____

YOUR HEADQUARTERS FOR HISTORY

WHOHQ
®

Who? What? Where?

www.whohq.com